Other books by Wilferd A. Peterson

The Art of Living (1961)
The New Book of the Art of Living (1963)
More About the Art of Living (1966)

A FOURTH BOOK

Adventures in the

OF NEW ESSAYS

Art of Living

by

WILFERD A. PETERSON

SIMON AND SCHUSTER · NEW YORK

Published by Simon and Schuster
Rockefeller Center, 630 Fifth Avenue
New York, New York 10020

First printing

Library of Congress Catalog Card Number: 68-22971
Designed by Richard C. Karwoski
Manufactured in the United States of America
Printed by United Lithographing Corp., New York

To my wife, Ruth, who is my partner in writing the Art of Living *books, and to the more than a million readers across the country and around the world*

Acknowledgment

My thanks to Dr. Willis H. Kinnear, editor of Science of Mind *Magazine, for permission to use and adapt a number of my writings which have appeared in his publication.*

He is the true artist whose life is his material; every stroke of the chisel must enter his own flesh and bone and not grate dully on the marble.

—Henry David Thoreau

CONTENTS

I THE ADVENTUROUS ATTITUDE

The Adventurous Attitude 13

II THE ADVENTURE OF SELF

You Are an Adventure 16
Vertical Living 17
The Balanced Self 18
Your Power to Be 20
Happy New You 21

III THE ADVENTURE OF PEOPLE

The Art of the Impossible 23
The Wave of a Hand 24
Search for a Perfect Tune 26
Declaration of Dependence 27
We Are the Decent People of the World 29

IV THE ADVENTURE OF IDEAS

Ideas Make Men Giants 31
Mind Alive 33
Perpetual Mental Motion 34
The Kingdom of Ideas 36
Skylight Thinkers 37

V THE ADVENTURE OF NATURE

Background for Man 39
The Pine Trees Talk 41
Prayer of an Outdoor Man 42
Mountains and Men 43
Secret of Serenity 44
The Peace of Nature 46

VI THE ADVENTURE OF AMERICA

The Land 48
The Founders 49
The Pioneers 51
The Builders 52
The Traditions 53
He Who Shoots the Stars 55

VII THE ADVENTURE OF THE SPIRIT

Heroes of Inner Space 56
Dynamic Good Will 57
Slow Me Down, Lord 58
Your Spiritual Ancestors 59
Key Words of the Spirit 61
God Is Alive 62

I

THE ADVENTUROUS ATTITUDE

Who never walks save where he sees men's tracks, makes no discoveries.
—J. G. Holland

The Adventurous Attitude

The key to unlocking the treasures in the art of living, the secret of adding new dimensions to your life, is simply this: *Hold an adventurous mental attitude.*

When you look at even the humdrum with an adventurous attitude, you infuse things with the brilliant light of newness. The dull becomes bright. The darkness is lighted up. You cannot become bored when you approach *everything* as an adventure! Think adventure!

Go forth seeking adventure. Open your eyes, your ears, your mind, your heart, your spirit and you'll find adventure *everywhere*. It is always there if you look for it. It is in your daily work, whether you are keeping books, making sales, teaching school, building bridges, driving a truck. . . . There is adventure in marriage, in having a child, in getting a meal. . . . There is adventure even in the disagreeable and fearful: in going to the dentist, in facing an operation. . . .

There is adventure in giving the speech you are afraid to give. Think of whatever you are doing as an adventure and watch your life change for the better. Adventure adds an aura of excitement.

Adventure begins with you, personally. It is in the way you look at things. It is the mental stance you take as you face your day. It is finding magic in things. It is talking with people and discovering their inner goodness. It is the thrill of feeling a part of the life around you.

The attitude of adventure will open things up for you. The world will come alive with new zest and meaning. You'll become more aware of the beauty everywhere. Nothing will seem unimportant. Everything will be revealed as having pattern and purpose.

The adventurous attitude will make you a discoverer. Things that were hidden will come into focus. Wonders to which you were blind will suddenly reveal themselves to you. The mysteries will unfold into revelations. The simple things will give forth their secrets.

The adventurous attitude will stretch your horizons. You will dare to travel to new places, to discover the world. In A.D. 430, Saint Augustine wrote: "The world is a great book and they who never stir from home read only a page." With the adventurous attitude you'll be inspired to turn the pages of many lands, to explore whole continents, to become a citizen of the world.

The adventurous attitude will challenge you to take the risk, to do that which is different, unknown. When you dare more, you will do more. The adventurous attitude frees you from fear, frees you to live. "A ship in harbor is safe, but that is not what ships are made for," wrote John Shedd. Life is for adventuring!

The adventurous attitude will keep you young. It will fill you with enthusiasm and the joy of being alive. You'll forget yourself in the glory of each new day.

The adventurous attitude is creative. It sends you forth in quest of new ideas, approaches, methods, principles, to build a better life here on earth. Life is never good enough as it is when you have the adventurous attitude. You are always probing, experimenting, exploring in search of ways to lift and improve life. Problems and projects are transformed into gallant crusades.

When you have an adventurous attitude you walk with God. Your consciousness expands. What was ordinary becomes extraordinary. What was common becomes uncommon. The ground on which you stand is holy ground!

When you have an adventurous attitude you seek adventure not only without, but also within. You seek to find out who you are, where you came from, what you are here for, and how you relate to other people and to the universe. You adventure deep within yourself.

The adventurous attitude is the way to face death as well as life. When the British steamship, the *Lusitania,* was torpedoed and sunk during the First World War, Charles Frohman spoke a few words to his companions on the slanting decks of the doomed ship. "Why fear death?" he said. "It is the most beautiful adventure in life."

The adventurous attitude resurrects man's ideals; it raises hope from the grave and sings a song of triumph. It is enduring, eternal, everlasting. It is the immortal quality in man that can never be defeated. It goes on forever.

Body: When the body slumps, so do mind and spirit. To be physically vertical suggests the soldier at attention, radiating courage, daring, force and energy. Of a dynamic woman it was said, "She walks like a queen." Straighten up and your mind will straighten out. An erect body lifts the thoughts.

Mind: Vertical thinking means maintaining an upward direction of thought. "Life consists of what a man is thinking *all day*," said Emerson. And Frank Channing Haddock commanded: "Live in the upper level of your mind!"

Spirit: As a television or radio antenna stretches upward to capture symphonies from the sky, so you, through meditation and prayer, can stretch your spirit upward to receive God's immortal music in your life. To be spiritually vertical means to keep constantly stretching upward toward life's highest good—toward love, faith, courage, hope and joy.

The zenith cannot be reached in a single leap. But, like the vertical line, you can constantly and persistently maintain your upward direction. Keep in mind the words of Browning: "Ah, but a man's reach should exceed his grasp, Or what's a heaven for?"

The Balanced Self

The man walks out on the high wire over empty space, sways above the breathless crowd, defies the law of gravity. . . .

The successful living of a life can be compared to walking across a high wire.

The indispensable quality needed is *balance*.

The balanced self is the well-integrated self. A harmonious combination of all the constructive elements of personality makes the self *whole*.

The balanced self practices moderation, avoids extremes, follows the maxim "Not anything too much."

The balanced self meets the vicissitudes of life with equanimity. It is neither exalted by success nor dejected by failure. It meets despair with hope and climbs the heights with humility.

The balanced self maintains mental equilibrium. It has ideals without illusions. It separates fact from fancy. It keeps a level head.

The balanced self is mature. It considers everything from a grown-up viewpoint balanced by a child's simplicity.

The balanced self balances dreams with action. It uses the power of inner thought to inspire outer achievement. And it uses action to stimulate further dreams.

The balanced self guards against quick emotional reactions. It does not jump to impulsive conclusions. It delays action until it has had time, calmly and fairly, to balance all the factors involved.

The balanced self is resilient; it is flexible to change. Like a tree in the wind, it bends without breaking.

The balanced self knows the error of constant effort. It renews itself through prayer and relaxation, that it may apply a higher impact of energy and creative power to the task at hand.

The balanced self lives a balanced life. It balances work and play, love and worship.

The balanced self maintains the I AM of the spirit at the center of self, in full command of its destiny.

Your Power to Be

"What you are," wrote Emerson, "thunders so loud I can't hear what you say to the contrary."

You radiate what you are! You go forth to others in love, in hate, in indifference, in warmth, in coldness, in cheer or in gloom. What you truly are, deep down inside, thunders silently as you meet and mingle with people.

The greatest sculptor is not Rodin or Michelangelo. The greatest sculptor is life.

You sculpture yourself into what you are by your dominant thoughts and acts. "Upon every face is written the life the man has lived," wrote Elbert Hubbard, "the prayers, the aspirations, the disappointments, all he had hoped for and was not–nothing is hidden or indeed can be."

What you are today is the result of the life you've lived up to this moment. What you will be tomorrow depends upon the quality of your life from now on. None of us is a finished product. We are each in the continual process of creating ourselves anew.

Your life emphasis should not be on possessing but on *becoming*. You should concentrate not on how you can have more, but how you can *be more*. The way in which you apply your *power to be* will determine what you *are*.

Your greatest power is your *power to be*. To be more loving. To be more courageous. To be more joyous. To be more friendly. To be more sensitive. To be more aware. To be

more forgiving. To be more tolerant. To be more humble. To be more patient. To be more helpful. . . . *To be a greater human being.*

You only achieve identity by being the best of whatever you have it in you to be, by giving full expression to your own unique spirit, to your own ideals and values, to your own gifts and talents, to your own concepts of beauty and truth.

Your power to be finds fulfillment as you relate to others. Giving of the self enlarges the self, helps you to be more. What you become, through your power to be, is mirrored in the eyes of others as the man you are.

To *be more* is the supreme adventure of being.

Happy New You

The conventional Happy New Year approach is to think of the New Year as something that happens outside of ourselves. It is a good luck wish that the New Year, in some magical way, will bring us our heart's desire. We look to the New Year to make us happy.

When we expect happiness to come to us from the *outside* we are usually disappointed. Happiness is not guaranteed by sunny weather, a raise in pay, a new car, a beautiful home or anything else of a material nature. External things are often possessed by very unhappy people.

Happiness does not come out of a New Year, it comes out of men and women. Life does not change when we hang a new calendar on the wall or when the clock strikes midnight and a New Year begins. The only way life will change for us is when we *change ourselves.*

The source of happiness is not in events happening outside of us; the source of happiness is *within us*. We cannot control the outside world but we can control our own thoughts and emotions. All true happiness is an *inner* experience.

There is a new phrase to speak to each other as we face the adventure of a New Year . . . *"Happy New You!"*

The way to make the New Year the best year of your life is to look to *yourself*, not to the year, for your happiness. . . .

To realize that happiness does not depend on the birth of a New Year, but on the birth of a New You.

To know that the months, weeks, days, hours and minutes of the New Year are empty until *you* fill them with happiness.

To face the fact that time is dead until you give it life, and that your happiness depends on the quality of life you give it.

Happy New You!

III

THE ADVENTURE OF PEOPLE

Create a great people, the rest follows.

—Walt Whitman

The Art of the Impossible

Adventure releases power in people. An adventurer is a positive thinker with *drive.*

Adventure is a compelling motivation for man's work, a shining star for which to reach.

Adventure is an alarm-clock word that wakes a man up and propels him into action.

Adventure is the lure of the strange, the unknown, the unexplored. It sent Columbus forth on his historic voyage, it inspired the Wright brothers to fly, it discovered radium, it settled the western plains, it harnessed electricity. . . .

Adventure is the force behind progress. Adventurers are unafraid of new ideas, new approaches, new ways of doing things. They try out new ideas, work for them, pioneer for them, and make them realities in our lives.

Adventure has inspired giant steps forward. Pile up all the achievements of man and you will have a towering monument to adventure. Civilization is the result of man's adventuring.

"The life of the adventurer," said Charles XII of Sweden, "is the practice of the art of the impossible." All through history the adventurer has wrestled with the things others said could not be done; he has faced scorn and ridicule and courageously held to his purpose. He has gloried in changing the world in thousands of ways to make it a better place for man.

The adventurer agrees with Napoleon, who said, "The word 'impossible' is found only in the dictionary of fools."

The spirit of adventure has created the world we live in today, and it will create the world we will live in tomorrow.

There will always be adventurers to lead us into a larger future.

Adventure makes men and nations great.

The Wave of a Hand

Not only with the magician, but with the common man, the wave of a hand works wonders.

Behind the iron curtain, as our bus followed the narrow lonely roads of the countryside, we waved our hands to the people, and ideologies, prejudices, fears and language barriers disappeared.

A girl walked across a meadow, driving a flock of sheep. She saw us, looked up in amazement, because few buses came that way. As we waved, her face lighted up, she smiled and waved back to us.

Coming our way was a crude wagon pulled by a team of oxen. The face of the driver was dull and expressionless. As we waved, he stared at us for an instant, then his face broke into a grin and he returned our waves.

A man on a donkey, his long legs almost touching the ground, his face set in grim lines, rode along the side of the road. We waved to him. He straightened up, looked our way and waved.

A boy driving a herd of cows passed in front of our bus, so the driver had to pull up and stop. We smiled and waved to the boy; surprised, he paused for a moment, then waved back.

People gathered in the village squares watched our bus with curiosity as it passed. As we waved, there came what seemed to be flashes of recognition and many raised their hands to wave to us.

In thousands of miles of travel, as we waved to the people, the great majority waved their hands in greeting to us.

The wave of a hand made us all kin! Spirit spoke to spirit, mind to mind. We saluted each other for our common humanity.

The people, suppressed by tyrants, their countries overrun by many conquerors, the Romans, the Huns, Napoleon, the thundering armies of Hitler, somehow retain their love of man for man. Crushed to earth, the spirit of brotherhood rises again.

The wave of a hand, and like an electric shock we suddenly realize that all men are one . . . that we share a common destiny . . . that we are sons of God . . . that we are brothers.

Wars come and go. Dictators rise and fall. Armies march and disappear. Cities are destroyed and rebuilt. But always men are the same—they hunger for the friendly gesture, they long for love and peace, they respond to the good.

The wave of a sword is a symbol of war; the wave of a hand is a universal symbol of the peace which all men want.

Search for the Perfect Tune

A vagabond went forth in search of the perfect tune. For many years he roamed the world. Here and there he discovered perfect notes, and he strung them together as he went on his way. . . .

From a bluebird singing its heart out at dawn.

From the thundering music of a waterfall.

From an old man playing his fiddle in front of his mountain cabin.

From a mother singing a lullaby to the child in her arms.

From a little brook babbling over the rocks.

From the voices of children singing in a choir.

From raindrops drumming on the roof.

From a gentle wind rustling the leaves of trees. . . .

There came the day when the vagabond was satisfied. He had gathered the notes he needed, and he set about to create the perfect tune.

When the perfect tune was finished, he took it to a great

orchestra that his masterpiece might be presented to a waiting world by the finest musicians.

All the musicians agreed that the tune was perfect, but no one agreed as to how it should be rendered.

The violins wanted more emphasis. The cymbals and the drums wanted their parts stressed. The woodwinds and the brass failed to see eye to eye about the relative importance of their parts.

The orchestra leader and his players could not agree on how the perfect tune should be interpreted.

And so the perfect tune was never played.

The world knows the perfect tune for harmony and peace among men. There is no secret about it. It is as old as the ages. Seers, prophets and sages have extolled it. The perfect tune is the expression of love and good will.

All that is needed is that men transcend their differences so that the perfect tune may be played on the heartstrings of all people everywhere.

Declaration of Dependence

This is my Independence Day Declaration of Dependence.

My hat is off to all the men and women everywhere upon whom I depend for life, liberty and the pursuit of happiness:

To miners risking their lives in the deep dark dungeons beneath the earth.

To airline pilots soaring over mountain peaks.

To actors, circus clowns and singers of grand opera.

To research experts fighting death and conquering new frontiers in the battle against disease.

To farmers toiling under the blazing sun.

To policemen and fire fighters.

To the faithful postman making his daily rounds.

To the barber who cuts my hair.

To the tailor who makes my clothes.

To teachers who show the way and to preachers who lift the spirit.

To writers of poems and makers of books.

To artists who fill the world with beauty through painting and music.

To the builders of highways.

To the milkman making his deliveries in the quiet hours of the morning.

To painters, garage men, electricians and plumbers.

To physicians and dentists, chemists and carpenters.

To street cleaners, telephone-repair men and gardeners.

To good cooks, philosophers and prophets.

To butchers, bakers and candlestick makers. . . .

To the endless list of people everywhere who create and operate the magic modern world in which I live, I give my eternal gratitude.

But for you I would be as helpless as Robinson Crusoe on his deserted island.

I would be a naked outcast in a wilderness of confusion.

No man is independent! We go riding through life on the shoulders of others.

So this is my Declaration of Dependence.

We Are the Decent People of the World

We are the decent people of the world.

We are in the majority, for men and women are essentially decent.

We live in all nations, we live under all the flags that fly.

Decency is not determined by our economic status, our religion, the language we speak, the color of our skin, or the ideology under which we live. Human decency is a universal quality.

We, the decent people of the world, often have our voices drowned out by the shouts of leaders who misrepresent the things for which we stand.

We the decent people carry enough weight to tip the scale for decency if we will make ourselves heard. . . .

We believe that war is the great indecency, that it kills and destroys all the higher sensibilities of man and leaves only death, suffering and destruction in its wake.

We believe that this is a beautiful universe and that it is made for love and not for hate; for peace and not war; for freedom and not slavery; for order and not riot; for compassion and not violence; for happiness and not misery.

We believe that there is only one war to be waged in the name of human decency, and that is the war against all the common enemies of man . . . hunger, disease, poverty, ignorance, crime and failure.

We believe that every child should have the chance to grow up in an atmosphere of faith, not of fear.

We believe that the ultimate decency is to help men and never harm men, to lift men and not degrade men, and to respect the dignity of all men as individual human beings.

We the decent people of the world stand for the kind of life that will be good for all of the people, all of the time, everywhere.

IV

THE ADVENTURE OF IDEAS

Ideas are weapons. A thinker has far more power than a dynamiter. Dreamers are the world shakers. With the song of a poet an empire may be trampled down . . . or built up.

—Thomas Dreier

Ideas Make Men Giants

Gutzon Borglum became a giant among sculptors because he conceived the daring idea of carving American leaders on a mountain.

He carved the giant figures of Washington, Jefferson, Lincoln and Theodore Roosevelt on Mount Rushmore in the Black Hills of South Dakota.

Before these men became giant figures on a mountain they were first giants of thought. Their ideas made them giants.

Washington had the audacious idea that he could lead his ragged little army to victory against the trained troops of the mighty British Empire; Jefferson expressed the idea of human freedom in one of the greatest documents ever written, the Declaration of Independence; Lincoln rose to greatness on the idea that our government could not permanently

endure half slave and half free; Theodore Roosevelt was inspired into whirlwind action for his country by the idea that aggressive fighting for the right is the greatest sport in the world.

"Creative personalities," wrote the historian Arnold J. Toynbee, "are the determining factor in history." The men with the great ideas are the giants.

In history, sculpture, art, literature, science, invention, business, philosophy, religion—in every area of life—the size of the man is judged by the size of his ideas.

First comes the adventure of sparking ideas to light the fuse . . . then comes the explosion of action.

No man can make others think unless he himself is a thinker. He can drop his ideas into other minds until, as a drop of red dye will tint a whole cask of water, his thoughts will influence civilization.

"Ideas that rouse and set multitudes to thinking," wrote A. Owen Penney, "come as gold from the mines."

The Master of Men proclaimed the law of love for God and love for man. He was nailed to a cross, but His great idea is eternal and will gain momentum through the ages.

A great idea stretches a man's mind into greatness, stretches his life into usefulness, stretches his spirit until he feels ten feet tall.

The bigness of your life, now and forever, will be measured by the size of your ideas.

Mind Alive

Mental aliveness means seeking the building blocks of ideas from every available source.

"Invention, strictly speaking," wrote Sir Joshua Reynolds, the English portrait painter, "is little more than a new combination of those images which have been previously gathered and deposited in the memory. Nothing comes of nothing. He who has laid up no material can produce no combinations."

Ideas may blossom suddenly, but only if the seed has been sown. There is no harvest from barren soil. The more alive a man's mind is, the more he has to work with in creating ideas.

A man should have a hungry mind. He should increase the scope of his reading, explore new areas, enlarge his perspective.

A man should learn to listen. He should sit at the feet of the masters who have made their marks in many fields of endeavor.

A man should immerse himself in life. He should mingle with crowds, rub shoulders with other men, travel the world.

A man should have a retreat, a cabin in the woods or a study in his home, where he may be alone to think and meditate. "The subconscious self," wrote Frank Channing Haddock, "requires aloneness and opportunity for silence. Let every article in your room suggest will, resourcefulness, power, success. Pictures on the walls of men admired. Books on the shelves full of inspiration. Music. Thus you suggest uplift and harmony for positive thought. You keep your

mind on the track without a sense of urge or drive. You stir your vast powers of inventiveness. You make yourself a mental powerhouse."

A man should keep close to nature. He should walk and think. He should ponder great ideas such as space illimitable, time everlasting, energy inexhaustible. He should mentally explore the universe.

A man should let his imagination play with the ten most beautiful words in the English language as listed by the famous lexicographer Wilfred J. Funk: dawn, hush, lullaby, murmuring, tranquil, mist, luminous, chimes, golden, melody. He should have an eye and an ear for beauty.

A man should preserve records of the great thoughts and ideas of other thinkers. He should keep scrapbooks, notebooks, files of material. He should begin the adventure of keeping a journal of his own daily thoughts and activities.

Being mentally alive is the process of saturating the mind with the stuff ideas are made of. It is the first vital step toward becoming an effective creative thinker.

Perpetual Mental Motion

When asked how he discovered the law of gravitation, Sir Isaac Newton replied, "By always thinking about it."

The master thinker keeps his mind in perpetual motion around the clock.

He never lets projects or problems out of his mind. He considers thinking a continuous adventure.

He uses the full scope of his mental powers. He fuses the surface level with the deeper level of his consciousness.

While the conscious level of his mind wrestles with a problem, the subconscious level continues to work on the many other problems he has turned over to it; its capacity is limitless.

He loafs creatively with one eye open for flashes of illumination. He has discovered that relaxation, not strain and stress, is the key to the free flow of ideas.

He does not confine his thinking to time spent at his desk. He knows that wherever he goes, his mind goes with him—that ideas are everywhere. His mind scans the universe as radar scans the skies.

He is constantly alert to the slightest intimation of an idea on any subject. He recognizes that many of the great ideas men have received have often come to them from areas far outside their regular daily work.

He is constantly alert to the significance of little things. He is aware that solutions to complex problems are often simple. He searches relentlessly for hidden clues to creation.

He knows that even while he sleeps, a part of his mind is awake, that his subconscious works as automatically as his heartbeat. He assigns work to this inner mind, knowing that during the night new concepts and patterns may be conceived to light the way to the answers he seeks.

He pictures his mind as a door always swung wide open, with the welcome sign out, inviting new ideas.

He knows that ideas are elusive and often quickly forgotten, so he traps them with notebook and pencil. He heeds the wise Chinese proverb: "The strongest memory is weaker than the palest ink."

He multiplies his power of achievement by keeping his mind at work twenty-four hours of each day.

The Kingdom of Ideas

To enter the Kingdom of Ideas, become as a little child.

"There is nothing more resembles God's eyes," wrote Nikos Kazantzakis, "than the eyes of a child."

A child has wide-eyed interest in everything. As God did, he looks upon the world and finds it good.

A child does not block the flow of goodness into his life by thoughts of fear and prejudice. His mind is as open as are his eyes. He experiences the wonder of life.

A child is an explorer. He is curious. He wants to know what is on the other side of the moon, or the room. He investigates things to find out what they are and how they work. He asks questions. He loves to experiment.

A child lives in the world of fantasy where all great ideas are born. It was probably a child who first dreamed of flying through the air, hearing voices and music from the sky, penetrating to the ocean depths. Before the reality comes the dream.

A child has the magic gift of imagination. He sees things that aren't there. He creates in his mind the kind of a world he wants to live in. He visualizes things as he wants them to be.

A child has freshness of response. To him the world is ever new and full of miracles and adventures. He reacts spontaneously to the discoveries he makes each day.

A child follows the simple way. He does not become bogged down in the complex and the obscure. He is natural, direct and genuine.

A child is confident. He has not learned all of the reasons why a thing cannot be done. He ignores obstacles because he does not know they exist.

This we learn from the child: The more childlike we are in our approach to problems, the more creative we will be. Try the fresh approach of a child.

Skylight Thinkers

Oliver Wendell Holmes defined the higher approach to creative thinking in this way: "There are one-story intellects, two-story intellects and three-story intellects with skylights. All fact collectors who have no aim beyond their facts are one-story intellects. Two-story men compare, reason, generalize, using the labors of the fact collectors as well as their own. Three-story men idealize, imagine, predict, their best illumination comes from above, *through the skylight.*"

Thomas Edison was a skylight thinker. "The key to successful methods," he said, "comes right out of the air. A real new thing like a general idea or a beautiful melody is pulled out of space."

Nikola Tesla never used a blueprint. His many inventions came to him through the skylight in complete visualizations.

Helmholtz, the renowned German scientist, said that his best ideas came to him as he walked under the open sky on a sunny day.

George Washington Carver asked God to tell him all about

the peanut. Through the skylight he received ideas on how to use the peanut to make over three hundred different products.

Walt Whitman's poems came through the skylight. He said, "I just let her come until the fountain is dry."

The novelist E. M. Forster explained that no matter what one's creative task may be, each of us start the process by gathering data and mentally working it over. As we work, something often happens, something comes to us that is normally beyond our reach. Mixed with the facts is a skylight factor that shapes the material into an inspiring idea. "When the process is over," wrote Forster, "when the picture, or lyric or novel (or whatever it is) is complete, the artist looking back on it will wonder how on earth he did it. And indeed he did not do it on earth."

The skylight factor is the secret of the genius.

Through quietness, meditation and prayer he keeps himself open to the flood of light from above.

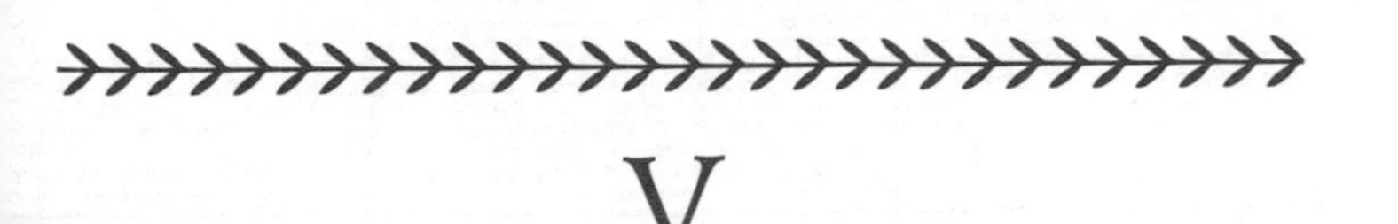

V

THE ADVENTURE OF NATURE

And this our life, exempt from public haunt,
Finds tongues in trees, books in the running brooks,
Sermons in stones, and good in every thing.
—Shakespeare

Background for Man

In diversity, complexity, surprise, wrath, serenity, destructiveness, magnificence, Nature's wild adventurous spirit is unexcelled.

From dainty rose to giant cactus, from ant to elephant, from fish to man, Nature is infinite in her scope.

Nature is sculptor, inventor, engineer, artist, architect, musician, friend and foe.

As sculptor Nature works on cliffs and canyon walls carving figures and towers, turrets and castles. Rock erosion is her chisel; rushing, pounding waters are her hammers.

As inventor Nature designs creatures that crawl, climb, leap, fly, jump, run, swim. They come in endless shapes,

sizes, coloring, with fins, fangs, feathers, claws, shells, feelers, stingers.

As engineer Nature creates a limitless universe with watch-like precision. She controls hundreds of billions of stars and their spinning planets. Time and tide, night and day, the flow of magnetic currents, light and air are under her command.

As artist Nature splashes color across the vast canvas of the sky with the radiance and splendor of sunrise and sunset. She arches rainbows against the passing storm, creates flowers and foliage, sets autumn woods on fire with the beauty of turning leaves and touches mountaintops with snow crystals.

As architect Nature builds pillars of clouds, rugged mountain ranges, deep canyons, quiet valleys and towering sky-scraper trees.

As musician Nature is maestro to ten thousand bird songs, chirping crickets, howl and roar of wild beasts, buzz of insects, trumpeting of elephants, organ music of the surf—the great symphony of forest and jungle.

As friend, Nature works as a creative partner with man, providing the gifts of soil, seed, sun, rain, minerals, chemicals—the forces, elements and ingredients for the preservation, perpetuation and evolution of life.

As foe, Nature sends floods, tornadoes, hurricanes, blizzards, sandstorms, earthquakes, relentless, devastating forces, to challenge and test man's will to conquer and survive.

Nature creates man's home on earth. It is a home of contrasts; of good and evil, beauty and ugliness, tranquility and terror. The whole natural world is the background against

which man plays his heroic part in the eternal adventure of his becoming.

The Pine Trees Talk

Have you ever listened to the pine trees?

Have they whispered to you their philosophy of life?

By a quiet lake in the moonlight I paused and listened, and this is what the pine trees said to me:

"We have grown tall, because we have grown straight.

"We have grown big because we have reached for the stars.

"We have learned that the way to increase our height is to keep growing.

"We have grown strong because we have rooted deep in the good earth.

"We have been patient, for we have learned that it takes time to grow a great tree.

"We have faced life bravely as it came, sunshine or storm, snow or rain.

"We have filled our sphere with the sweet aroma of our needles and have given shade to those who came our way.

"We have known the joy of service by sheltering with our branches the nests of birds.

"We have been still and listened to God, and we have seen His face in the dawning of each new day."

The pine trees were silent then, swaying as though in bene-

diction. I walked away beneath the stars meditating on their message.

Prayer of an Outdoor Man

With the leafy branches of the forest trees I lift my arms to pray; with the babbling brooks and singing birds I raise my voice in praise.

I thank Thee for the out-of-doors.

I thank Thee for old clothes, rough work and the right to let my beard grow.

I thank Thee for the curling smoke of my campfire in the early morning.

I thank Thee for steaming coffee, sizzling bacon and an outdoor appetite.

I thank Thee for the swish of my paddle and the joy of watching fleecy clouds roll by.

I thank Thee for silvery moonbeams on rippling water.

I thank Thee for the call of the whippoorwill at dusk across a quiet lake.

I thank Thee for the singing of my reel and the bending of my rod as a big one strikes.

I thank Thee for the contentment that comes with the patter of raindrops on my tent at night.

I thank Thee for wild blackberries along an old stump fence.

I thank Thee for my dogs, my gun, and the flaming colors of the autumn woods.

I thank Thee for wild ducks flying south against a dull gray sky.

I thank Thee for the glory and the majesty of the stars.

I thank Thee for strong winds pulling at my hair roots and for the spray from the lake on my cheeks.

I thank Thee for old trails, for rocks, for raging rapids, and for a glimpse of deer drinking in a secluded pool.

I thank Thee for the drum of the partridge, for squirrels, trailing arbutus, the aroma of pine needles, sunshine through the leaves, and all the other eternal miracles of the out-of-doors.

Mountains and Men

Mountains have always challenged men to climb them. Men have accepted the challenge, so few mountain peaks remain unconquered.

Mountain climbers soon discovered that one man alone is no match for a mountain. The lone climber often falls to his death.

Sir John Hunt, head of the expedition that reached the top of Mount Everest, told the secret of all successful climbing: "You get to the top of a mountain," he said, "only by climbing with other men on a rope."

The rope is the lifeline of the men who climb mountains.

It ties the men together so they can help each other climb.

When a man stumbles or falls, there are other men to save him.

When one man seeks handholds or footholds farther up, other men below him protect him by bracing themselves and standing firm and strong.

When the climbers in the lead reach a higher elevation, they use the rope to help the other men to climb up to where they are.

By climbing together on a rope men apply the combined power of their muscles and skills, their courage and confidence, to reach their mutual objective.

"Mountains," wrote Michael Roberts, "may be symbols or images of other reality."

Like mountain peaks, the unclimbed ideals of life challenge men.

One man alone cannot climb the mountain of world peace.

But there is no mental or spiritual mountain that cannot be scaled if men will climb together—if they will follow the philosophy of thc mountain climbers, protecting each other against falldowns and failures, lending a hand to help each other move upward, combining their talents and abilities, their faith and devotion.

The victorious ascent of a mountaintop ideal demands the tying together of the bodies, minds, hearts and spirits of men with the invisible rope of a common purpose.

Secret of Serenity

The ocean has many moods. Sometimes the colors of the sunrise are painted on the ocean surface as on a huge smooth canvas. At other times whitecapped waves thunder against the shore.

The surface of the ocean changes constantly. Now it is smooth and quiet. Again it becomes violent and tempestuous. But in its depths, down under the storms that whip the surface into a fury, there is a zone of eternal calm which no storm ever reaches, no hurricane ever ruffles.

The surface of life is also in a state of constant flux, with good days and bad, victory and defeat. To maintain, as the ocean does, a deep inner calm, while the storms of misfortune, reverses, fears and worries lash at the surface of life, is to discover the secret of serenity.

Years ago, when Thomas Edison's factory burned down, he wasted no time bemoaning his fate. Immediately after the disaster the reporters found a calm, quiet man already at work on plans for a new building.

When Emerson's home was destroyed by fire and his precious books were being reduced to ashes, Louisa May Alcott came to console him. The great philosopher said, "Yes, yes, Louisa, they are all gone, but let us enjoy the blaze now. Isn't it beautiful!"

Such men are ocean personalities. In their inner depths they are not defeated by what happens to them.

The towering waves of circumstances cannot reach us when we go deep within to seek the peace that passes all understanding. While the surface of life is in turmoil we can find an inner calmness to see us through.

Walt Whitman must have discovered this truth, for he wrote, "Nothing external to me can have any power over me."

The stillness of the ocean depths is a symbol of perfect poise.

The Peace of Nature

In a personal letter written from Africa in the Second World War, a flyer told what he saw while flying off on a bombing mission.

"Fluffy white clouds were piled up like great pillars in the sky," he wrote. "Below we caught glimpses of green fields. Arabs were tending their sheep down there oblivious to the war. Ahead of us were snowcapped mountains with sunbeam halos. Never before have I set eye on a more peaceful scene. How ironic to be observing the peace of nature while rushing on at 400 miles an hour toward the flak the enemy would soon be sending up at us!"

Wars come and wars go while brooks go babbling on their ageless way.

Thousands die on the battlefields while trees send out their leaves as they have been doing since time began.

Men fight each other in the sky where birds still sing their songs.

Villages and cities burn red against the night sky while the silent stars look on.

In nature there is eternal, permanent peace. Man alone breaks himself against the laws of God.

How long, O God, how long must men live on this planet before they learn that war causes all to lose and none to gain, and that peace and happiness are won only through understanding, brotherhood and good will?

All *is* well with the world! It offers us the tools and materials of peace and prosperity. The rich soil invites the seeds.

Trees and rocks and minerals are ready for the hands of builders and creators. New chemical elements await discovery.

In our hands we have the building blocks of heaven on earth. Why do we create the hell of war?

VI

THE ADVENTURE OF AMERICA

I believe that America is the best hope of man.

—Frank Yerby

The Land

Scoop up a handful of soil and hold in your hand the miracle that is America.

The precious grains of sand reflect a nation of contrasts.

The unlimited horizons of sweeping plains, burning deserts and rolling prairies.

The tranquility of snug harbors, quiet villages and shining inland lakes.

The energy of thundering waterfalls, roaring cities and the flaming sky of steel mills.

The neighborliness of old rail fences, railroads and highways tying a nation together.

The challenge of snowcapped mountains and giant trees towering into the sky.

The laughter of merry little brooks dancing their way to the sea.

The promise of the deep, straight furrows of the plowman.

The bounty of vast fields of waving grain.

The power of mighty waves pounding a rockbound coast.

The inspiration of the lights of a great city at night seen from the window of an airplane.

The silence of the everlasting stars.

This is America.

This is the land we love.

The Founders

They were men of destiny building foundations under mankind's long dream of freedom.

There was Thomas Jefferson writing the most inspired words ever to flash from the mind of man: "We hold these truths to be self-evident, that all men are created equal, that they are endowed by their Creator with certain inalienable rights, that among these are Life, Liberty and the pursuit of Happiness. . . ."

The Declaration of Independence set into motion a gospel of equality, of natural rights and of government by the consent of the governed that raised all men to a new level of dignity.

There was John Hancock, who wrote his name first in poster letters, on the Declaration of Independence and then stood back and said, "I guess King George can read that without spectacles."

There was a tall, great-hearted man, who arose in the Virginia Assembly and said, "I will raise a thousand men and arm and subsist them at my own expense and march to the relief of Boston." His name was George Washington.

There was gallant Thomas Paine, who during the dark days at Valley Forge wrote these flaming words: "These are the times that try men's souls. 'Tis the business of little minds to shrink; but he whose heart is firm and whose conscience approves his conduct will pursue his principles unto death."

There was Samuel Adams, who, when someone expressed the fear that the British would destroy our seaport towns if we antagonized them, replied, "Our towns are built of brick and wood; if they are burned we can rebuild them; but liberty once gone is gone forever."

There was dynamic young Alexander Hamilton, master of organization and dispatch, who helped establish the machinery of the new government.

There was the old patriarch, Benjamin Franklin, who stood up before the Constitutional Convention to suggest that the Divine Providence that watches over the fall of a sparrow was certainly interested in the rise of a new nation and that we should turn to that source for help.

Out of the faith, work and sacrifice of our heroic founders grew a federal government that respects the sovereignty of the states, yet secures its sanction and power directly from the people.

The Pioneers

America owes much to men who pushed on to new horizons—to Kit Carson, Daniel Boone, David Crockett, old Jim Bridger, and others of their stamp and kind. They were men as big as the country, as broad as the plains, as tall as the mountains. They took America in their rugged hands and stretched it from sea to shining sea.

The pioneers drove their covered wagons into the setting sun, they poled their rafts down the rivers, they walked afoot through the forest with long rifles in readiness. The ring of the ax of the pioneer was the ring of freedom moving on.

There were brave women among the pioneers—women leaving the security of the known for the mystery of the unknown; women leaving their families and friends for the loneliness of plain and prairie; for the dangers of the vast unsettled wilderness, with the nearest neighbor fifty miles away.

The spirit of the pioneers is the spirit that has made America great. They knew the fellowship of hardship, the comradeship of common problems.

The New England Yankee with his nasal twang, the Carolinian with his Southern drawl, men of many faiths and backgrounds, met and mingled and helped each other.

The frontier inspired self-confidence and pride in achievement. It taught the value of dogged perseverance. It destroyed the veneer of artificiality, and men became simple, sincere and genuine.

"Root hog or die" . . . "Get up and git" . . . "Find a way or make one." In such phrases we catch the conquering cour-

age of the pioneers. They were dissatisfied with things as they were. They had the urge to move on. Their faces were toward the future.

The Builders

Over the trails blazed by the frontiersmen came the men with plows, the seekers of homes in the wilderness, the builders.

They cleared out the underbrush, felled trees, notched logs and built cabins; they laid rail fences around their lands.

They planted and raised corn, beans, turnips, cabbages, potatoes.

The women mastered a hundred arts to make the humblest house a home. They weaved, quilted, made soap and candles, sewed clothes, cooked over an open fire and cared for a growing family. And when danger threatened, the hand that rocked the cradle could also shoot a gun.

Neighbors worked together to open roads through the woods and to build rough wooden bridges over streams.

As increasing numbers of people came, the settlements grew. Meetinghouses, blacksmith shops, stores, churches, saloons, schools, dance halls, and forts for protection against Indian attacks appeared on the horizon of the empty land.

Then came law and government with courthouses and log jails.

Printing presses were hauled in over deserts and mountains, and frontier newspapers began to appear.

The settlers put down deep roots, and the storms of a thousand difficulties could not tear them loose from their dynamic faith in the future of a growing America.

The settlements became villages, and the villages stretched themselves into cities.

Log cabins became skyscrapers, wooden bridges became webs of steel and concrete spanning wide rivers.

Covered wagons and stagecoaches gave way to railroads, automobiles and airplanes.

Candles in the windows of cabins became the glow of hundreds of brilliantly lighted Main Streets.

Free men, fused together in a common purpose, built, under God, a new and mighty nation on the earth.

The Traditions

When we think about the traditions of the land we love, a thousand thoughts flash in our minds, trailing clouds of glory. . . .

America, simple and sublime, heroic and humble, trivial and great, demands recording.

The midnight ride of Paul Revere and "the shot heard 'round the world."

Old Ironsides, clipper ships, sidewheelers on the Mississippi and a lighthouse on the rockbound coast of Maine.

George Washington and the cherry tree, and Abe Lincoln writing figures on a shovel before an open fire.

Grandfather clocks, the little red schoolhouse, and the church in the valley by the wildwood.

Log cabins and the White House, the Virginia reel and "Turkey in the Straw."

Potbellied stoves and cracker-barrel discussions in the country store.

The band concert in the village square, bicycles built for two, hitching posts and the "one-hoss shay."

The pony express, stagecoaches, wagon trains and Indian wigwams.

The lonely whistle of a locomotive crossing the prairie at night; the driving of the golden spike; and the gathering of people at train time at the village depot.

Fort Ticonderoga, the Alamo, and Sousa leading his band in "The Stars and Stripes Forever."

Columbus and the Santa Maria, Plymouth Rock and the Pilgrims, Pocahontas and John Smith.

Francis Scott Key writing "The Star Spangled Banner" "by the rockets' red glare," and Negroes on the Old Plantation singing "Swing Low, Sweet Chariot."

Mighty Paul Bunyan, legendary hero of the lumber camps, with Babe his Blue Ox, and Johnnie Appleseed planting apple trees across the nation.

The ring of the blacksmith's hammer, the Liberty Bell, Bunker Hill and Valley Forge.

Precious documents preserved for posterity: The Declaration of Independence, The Constitution, The Bill of Rights and Lincoln's Gettysburg Address.

The riches of the American heritage defy recording by the voices and pens of men; they are as high as our mountains, as deep as our seas, as wide as our plains; they quicken the pulse and lift the spirit; they touch us and leave us with a prayer of thankfulness in our hearts.

*He Who Shoots the Stars**

I am Pumunangwet, He Who Shoots the Stars!
I symbolize the spirit of America;
My eyes search the heavens of our greater destiny;
My bow twangs a symphony of conquest;
Each singing arrow seeks a higher star!

I am Pumunangwet, Inspirer of Men!
I am the Challenge of the Unachieved;
I am fear conquered and Courage crowned King;
I am the call to High Adventure;
I am the Forward Look and the Upward Reach;
My war cry sounds from the highest cliff;
My flaming arrows point the way to goals
yet unattained!

I am Pumunangwet, Chief of the Conquerors!
I ask all daring men to join my tribe;
I ask that you fit arrows to your bows;
The sky is full of stars to shoot. . . .
The stars of Plenty, Happiness and Peace;
The Upward March of man has but begun,
So bend your bows and let the arrows fly!

* The above poem was inspired by Philip Sears' bronze statue of an Algonquin brave called Pumunangwet (He Who Shoots the Stars) and is dedicated to the sculptor.

VII

THE ADVENTURE OF THE SPIRIT

Just as a candle cannot burn without a fire, men cannot live without a spiritual life.

—Buddha

Heroes of Inner Space

The heroes of outer space have their sights set on exploring new worlds in the universe. The objective of the heroes of inner space is to discover how to save the world in which we now live.

Targets of the heroes of outer space are the moon, Mars and beyond! Target of the heroes of inner space is the human heart and how to reach it and change it.

The heroes of inner space are exploring the vast unknown spaces within man; they are delving into his unconscious motivations, his habit patterns, his instincts, his spiritual potentialities, his relationship to the eternal.

The heroes of inner space recognize that everything that goes on in the world begins inside the minds of men. Man's

survival depends on the man *inside*. The thoughts he thinks create the world he lives in. He makes the decisions, he gives the commands.

The heroes of inner space are creative heroes. They lead the way into new areas, they open up new vistas, they are the discoverers of new ways to long-sought goals. They are spiritual adventurers.

To build more lift into rockets is the goal of the heroes of outer space; to build more lift into man's consciousness is the aim of the heroes of inner space.

The heroes of inner space work their heroics within the minds and hearts of men. You can't see a great thought, but often it has more impact than a nuclear missile. Inner heroism is invisible but it is the greatest heroism of all.

In a sky full of planes, missiles and rockets, let us leave room for man's soaring thoughts and aspirations. Let us give wings to the spirit of man.

The heroes of inner space are those who send great ideas and ideals into orbit around the earth.

Dynamic Good Will

God's will and *good will* are synonymous terms. If we strive to express good will in our lives, we express God's will, for certainly God wills only good for His world. By serving as channels for the spirit of good will we become dynamic partners with God.

Good will is not a single quality. It is a composite of *all* the qualities of the spirit, applied to daily living.

When one expresses good will he includes love, faith, tolerance, hope, joy, courage, patience and all the other constructive values.

Good will is also the complete antidote for all mental poisons; it overcomes hate, envy, jealousy. When one turns on good will in his mind, these and all other negatives disappear, as darkness disappears when you switch on a light.

Good will may be compared to potential and kinetic electrical energy. As potential energy, good will represents a tremendous untapped power for good. As kinetic energy, good will represents the power for good activated and set into motion in the lives of individuals.

Good will is the will to live the good life. It is a dynamic directional drive toward goodness.

Good will is a power that can be used every day of the year and every hour of the day. It is instantly available. By continuously practicing good will we cultivate a deep subconscious habit of good will. It becomes the pattern of our response in all situations.

Good will works as silently as the sun and with as much power. It thaws the ice and snow of resistance and indifference. It warms and wins human hearts. It draws forth the best in others as flowers are drawn from the soil. It stimulates growth.

Men can use the dynamic power of good will to create a new world.

Slow Me Down, Lord

Slow me down, Lord! Ease the pounding of my heart by the

quieting of my mind. Steady my hurried pace with a vision of the eternal reach of time.

Give me, amidst the confusion of my day, the calmness of the everlasting hills. Break the tensions of my nerves and muscles with the music of the singing streams which live in my memory.

Help me to know the magic restoring power of sleep.

Teach me the art of taking minute vacations . . . of slowing down to look at a flower, to chat with a friend, to pat a dog, to read a few lines from a good book.

Remind me each day of the fable of the hare and the tortoise, that I may know that the race is not always to the swift; that there is more to life than increasing its speed.

Let me look upward into the branches of the towering oak and know that it grew great and strong because it grew slowly and well.

Slow me down, Lord, and inspire me to send my roots deep into the soil of life's enduring values, that I may grow upward toward the stars of my greater destiny.

Your Spiritual Ancestors

Your physical ancestors were chosen for you before you were born. Factors such as the color of your skin, the color of your eyes, whether you are short or tall, are physical characteristics that were predetermined for you, and there isn't anything you can do about them.

But you can choose your spiritual ancestors!

Through books you can walk and talk with the great men

and women of the ages. By living close to them, by thinking their thoughts after them, their dreams, insights, principles and ideals may become a part of you.

The spiritual ancestors you select will guide you into a richer life.

Shakespeare will inspire you to make the most of yourself: "The fault, dear Brutus, is not in our stars, but in ourselves, that we are underlings."

Mark Twain will put a twinkle in your eye: "So live that when you come to die even the undertaker will be sorry."

Lincoln will broaden your sympathy: "With malice toward none; with charity for all. . . ."

Robert E. Lee will set you an example of forgiveness and forbearance, as set forth by his biographer Gamaliel Bradford: "His soul was tranquil and serene and broadly luminous, with no dark corner in it for violence or hate."

Jesus of Nazareth will direct you in your relations with men with the Golden Rule: "All things whatsoever ye would that men should do to you, do ye even so to them."

Buddha will emphasize the power of thought to control your life: "All we are is the result of what we have thought. The mind is everything. What we think we become."

George Washington Carver will suggest an attitude toward your daily work: "When you do the common things of life in an uncommon way, you will command the attention of the world."

Jane Addams will give you a new vision of time: "Our minds are stretched to the measure of the philosopher who

thinks of eternity not as duration of time but as a certain quality of soul which once obtained can never cease to exist."

You can claim the greatest spirits who ever lived as your spiritual ancestors. You can open yourself to the inspiration and challenge of their lives. You can bathe your mind in their high and noble thoughts. You can let their lives shine through you.

Key Words of the Spirit

There are two simple little words that are the very heart of the life of the spirit.

The first word is *Open*. Ralph Waldo Trine gave the secret of how to attune our lives to God. "The principal word to use is the word *Open,*" he wrote. "To be in tune with the Infinite you must simply *open* your heart and mind to the divine inflow which is waiting for the opening of the gate that it may enter."

To have an *open self* is to provide a free channel for the infinite goodness of God. To have an *open self* is to keep yourself aware, alert and sensitive to the beauty and wonder of life. God's love will flow through you into the world when you are *open*. You enlarge the dimensions of your life when you keep yourself *open* to the highest and best. The key to God's infinite riches is within you; *open* yourself and you will receive.

The second word is *One*. Dr. Charles Eliot of Harvard declared that the chief characteristic of the religion of the future will be man's recognition of his *oneness* with the great Creative Force of God, which finds its outlet through man himself.

"The life of the soul," said Emerson, "in conscious union with the Infinite shall be for thee the only real existence."

Beyond a conscious *oneness* with God you should also think of yourself as *one* with all men and all living things. All the men you have met and known are a part of you and you are a part of them forever. You cannot live separately and alone. You are one with the universe, with the sun, the sea and the stars. You are a part of all life, plant, animal, human and divine.

"To awaken into a vision of wholeness where we saw only fragments," wrote Horatio Dresser, "is to begin to have a philosophy of the spirit."

Open and *One* . . . two little words with life-changing power!

God Is Alive

God is alive, unfolding, evolving, expanding, changing. From single cells to solar system, in full circle without end, this is the everlasting life of God.

The poet Robert Frost distilled his philosophy into three words when he wrote, "Life goes on." Which is to say that God goes on, for God is life.

God is alive in flowers and snowflakes, in sunsets and rainbows, in the flash of lightning and the crash of thunder, in the calm in the eye of the hurricane. Wherever there is life there is God.

God is not far off on a throne in the sky; He is alive today in all men who walk the earth. He is the life that surrounds and penetrates us here and now. God is alive in man.

God is alive in the work of men. He creates masterpieces through men. He worked through the hammer and chisel of Michelangelo, the brushes of Rembrandt, the pen of Shakespeare, the illuminations of saints and sages. He inspires men to explore and discover, to invent and progress, to heal and save.

When we think and meditate we move in the infinite, and the life of God works *through us*. The consciousness of love, the sense of kinship, the flame of hope, the impulse to do good, the genius to create, this is God alive in you and me.

Jesus felt the power of God alive in him when he said ". . . the Father that dwelleth in me, he doeth the works." He expressed his mission in terms of the life of God when he said, "I have come that they might have life, and that they might have it more abundantly."

God is not a static image; he lives in everything and everyone. He is in the flight of an eagle and in the writing of a sonnet. He is everywhere. He is in the farthest star and the newborn baby. He will survive the denial of men and the blast of nuclear destruction.

Let us affirm the invincibility of God—for God is life eternal.

About the Author

Wilferd A. Peterson was born in Whitehall, Michigan, and spent his boyhood in Muskegon. He is a former Grand Rapids advertising executive, and has received the Silver Medal Award as advertising man of the year.

Mr. Peterson is also the recipient of the George Washington Medal from Freedom's Foundation at Valley Forge, "for outstanding achievement in bringing about a better understanding of the American way of life."

He is the author of the best-selling *Art of Living* books including three volumes published previous to this one: *The Art of Living* (1961), *The New Book of the Art of Living* (1963), and *More About the Art of Living* (1966). Together, the four volumes contain over a hundred different essays on the art of living.

He is a member of the Editorial Board of *Science of Mind* Magazine, for which he writes a monthly page, and is a member of the Advisory Board of *Sunshine* Magazine. He contributes to *Reader's Digest* and *This Week* Magazine.

He has addressed church congregations, service clubs and many other groups, and has appeared on radio and television.